The Washington Monument

A Tribute to a Man, a Monument for a Nation

The
Washington
Monument

A Tribute to a Man, a Monument for a Nation

 **Frederic Gilmore**

THE CHILD'S WORLD®, INC.

Library of Congress Cataloging-in-Publication Data
Gilmore, Frederic.
The Washington monument : a tribute to a man, a monument for a nation / by Frederic Gilmore.
p.   cm.
Includes index.
Summary: Describes the history of the Washington Monument,
how it was built, and what it represents.
ISBN 1-56766-760-0
1. Washington Monument (Washington, D.C.)—Juvenile literature.
[1. Washington Monument (Washington, D.C.) 2. National Monuments.]   I. Title.
F203.4. W3 G55   2000
975.3—dc21   99-086279

Credits

© Archive Photos: 20
© Bettmann/CORBIS: 9, 13, 15, 19, 24
© D.J. Ball/Tony Stone Images: 2
© Hulton Getty: 6, 16
© Jon Ortner/Tony Stone Images: 30
© Laurence Parent: 29
© North Wind Picture Archives: 10
© Peter Finger/CORBIS: 26
© Photophile/Bachmann: 23
© Tom Devol/Gnass Photo Images: cover

On the cover...

Front cover: One of the flags at the base of the Washington Monument waves in the breeze.
Page 2: Cherry trees blooming nearby make the monument seem even more beautiful.

In 1789, George Washington became the first president of the United States. As the president of a new nation, Washington saw a need for a city to house the people and the buildings of its government. Some people believed that the nation's capital should be Philadelphia. Others thought it should be Boston, while still others thought it should be New York.

Washington did not think any of these places was the best choice. He believed that the nation's capital should not be within any of the 13 states. Having the capital in a separate location would help keep the government from having **allegiance** to any one state.

⇐ **George Washington, first president of the United States.**

In 1791, the United States Congress chose a site for the capital city on the banks of the Potomac River. The capital city was to be called "Washington," named for President George Washington. The location of the city would be called "The District of Columbia," after the explorer Christopher Columbus.

Washington hired a French engineer and architect named Pierre Charles L'Enfant to design the capital city. L'Enfant's plan called for a capitol building, a presidential palace, and a large mall lined with all the offices of government. Along with all of these buildings, the plan called for a huge monument to honor the achievements of George Washington. The monument would recognize everything from his leadership of the Colonial Army to his role as first president of the United States.

Pierre Charles L'Enfant, designer of the city. ⇒

Work began on the new capital city in 1791. Three members of the new government's Continental Congress were chosen to oversee the construction. The congressmen and L'Enfant had many disagreements during the construction. Because of the disagreements, L'Enfant was fired in 1792. As a result, the plans for the capital city began to change.

Despite the changes, the plans for the city still included a monument to President Washington. The Congress had considered several ideas for the monument, but no one could agree on what it should look like or how big it should be. Work on the capital city continued, but debates over the monument went on for more than 40 years.

A Plan for a Monument

By 1833, Washington, D.C., still did not have a monument honoring the first president. The federal government had not been able to agree on a plan for building it. Finally, a group of people living in the area decided to come up with a plan of their own. The group called itself the Washington National Monument Society.

Congress gave the society permission to collect money for the monument's construction. Collection boxes were set up next to ballot boxes during elections. Although many Americans believed a monument should be built, few people had money to donate. Collecting enough money for a monument would take years.

Before the Monument Society, these lottery ⇒ tickets were sold to pay for the monument.

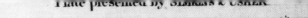

BALTIMORE

WASHINGTON MONUMENT LOTTERY
Third Class

The holder of this TICKET will be entitled to such PRIZE as may be drawn to its number if demanded within twelve months after completion of the drawing subject to a deduction of FIFTEEN PER CENT. Payable sixty days after conclusion   Baltimore June 1816

No_____   M_____

Plate presented by SIMKINS & USHER

BALTIMORE

WASHINGTON MONUMENT LOTTERY
Third Class

The holder of this TICKET will be entitled to such PRIZE as may be drawn to its number if demanded within twelve months after completion of the drawing subject to a deduction of FIFTEEN PER CENT. Payable sixty days after conclusion   Baltimore June 1816

No_____   M_____

Plate presented by SIMKINS & USHER

BALTIMORE

WASHINGTON MONUMENT LOTTERY
Third Class

The holder of this TICKET will be entitled to such PRIZE as may be drawn to its number if demanded within twelve months after completion of the drawing subject to a deduction of FIFTEEN PER CENT. Payable sixty days after conclusion   Baltimore June 1816

No_____   M_____

Plate presented by SIMKINS & USHER

BALTIMORE

WASHINGTON MONUMENT LOTTERY
Third Class

The holder of this TICKET will be entitled to such PRIZE as may be drawn to its number if demanded within twelve months after completion of the drawing subject to a deduction of FIFTEEN PER CENT. Payable sixty days after conclusion   Baltimore June 1816

No_____   M_____

As money was being collected, the members of the Washington National Monument Society began to look at plans. How big should the monument be? What should it look like? Robert Mills was a well-known architect at the time. He presented a plan that was based on L'Enfant's original idea for the monument.

Mill's' plan was for an **elaborate** circular building 100 feet tall and 250 feet across. The building would contain statues of Washington throughout his military career and presidency. Other areas in the building would have statues of famous people from the Revolutionary War. An **obelisk** tower 500 feet tall would stand on top of the building. It would be so tall that it could be seen from anywhere in Washington, D.C. The society was so impressed with Mills's idea, they accepted his plan.

This is Mills's early idea for the monument. ⇒
Notice the huge building at the base.

The society now faced another problem—they had collected only $87,000. With so little money, the society had to eliminate the circular building. They decided to build just the obelisk tower instead.

The base for the huge tower was built 36 feet down into the ground. The cornerstone of the building was put in place on July 4, 1848. The outside of the building was built with white **marble** from Maryland. The bottom of the building was a square more than 55 feet long on each side. The walls were 15 feet thick.

A Monument Unfinished

By 1854, work on the monument was going well, and the obelisk tower was 150 feet tall. Then a group called the **Know-Nothing Party** became the main influence to the Washington National Monument Society. The Know-Nothing Party had ideas that were not popular with the public.

Around the same time, a special piece of black marble donated by Pope Pius IX was stolen. Pope Pius IX had given the marble to be part of the decoration inside the monument. Many people believed that the Know-Nothing Party was responsible for the missing marble. Also during this time, problems began to arise between the northern and southern states. For all of these reasons, people stopped donating money to the society. Work on the monument slowly came to a stop between 1855 and 1858 due to the lack of money.

This drawing shows the monument just before ⇒ the first round of construction stopped.

At just over 150 feet tall, the monument to George Washington stood unfinished for years. By 1876, President Ulysses S. Grant grew unhappy that the monument was not finished. Grant asked the members of the Washington National Monument Society to give the unfinished building to the people of the United States. The society agreed to Grant's request. This made it possible for the federal government to pay for work done on the monument. Now the construction could continue.

Ulysses S. Grant, the 18th president
← **of the United States.**

A New Beginning

On August 2, 1878, work began again on the monument. The Army Corps of Engineers was put in charge of the construction, and the monument began to grow. But the years of no construction had left a mark on the monument. Even though the white marble now being used was from the same **quarry** in Maryland, it was a little darker in color. Today, you can see a ring on the monument about 150 feet above the ground where the two colors of marble meet.

If you look closely, you can see the two ⇒ colors of marble used on the monument.

Inside the monument, workers built a stairway to a viewing floor at the top. The stairway has 898 steps. "Memorial Stones" were built into the walls of the stairway. These stones were given to the National Monument Society and the Army Corps of Engineers to be included in the monument. The stones were gifts from states as well from people, organizations, and other nations around the world. The idea of the "Memorial Stones" was similar to the black marble stone donated by Pope Pius IX.

⇐ **This photo was taken looking straight up inside the monument. People are on the stairway (right).**

Construction of the monument continued until December 6, 1884. On that date, workers placed an aluminum **apex** on the top of the building, completing the monument. At 555 feet, 5⅛ inches high, the Washington Monument is the tallest **masonry** tower in the world.

A law was passed to keep people from building anything taller than 13 stories in Washington, D.C. This meant that no other building in the city would ever be as tall as the Washington Monument. The monument would always be able to be seen as the tallest building in the city.

⇐ **This drawing shows the project superintendent placing the tip on the capstone.**

On February 22, 1885, President Chester A. Arthur held a ceremony to open the Washington Monument. In 1888, the monument was opened to the public. An elevator was later added to make getting to the viewing floor easier. A circle of 50 American flags now surrounds the base of the monument. This circle is similar to Mills's original idea for the building.

Here you can see the flags that surround ⇒
the base of the monument.

In the years since, the Washington Monument has been the site of celebrations and ceremonies. It has also been the site of protests and rallies by groups of people expressing their views to our government.

The Washington Monument has become what Pierre L'Enfant hoped it would be. It is a monument to the great leader George Washington, and it is a widely recognized symbol of the capital of the United States of America.

Glossary

allegiance (uh–LEE–jenss)
Allegiance is commitment or loyalty to a person or government. George Washington wanted the nation's capital to be a separate place so the federal government wouldn't have an allegiance to any one state.

apex (AY–peks)
An apex is the top of an object that comes to a single point. An aluminum apex sits atop the Washington Monument.

elaborate (ee–LAB–or–et)
Something that is elaborate is worked on until it is very decorated or complex. Original plans for the Washington Monument called for a very elaborate building.

Know-Nothing Party (NO NU–thing PAR–tee)
The Know-Nothing Party was a group of people in the 1800s who did not like newcomers and Catholics in America. Some people blamed the Know-Nothing Party for the disappearance of a special stone given by Pope Pius IX.

marble (MAR–bull)
Marble is a type of stone that is very hard and good for building. The Washington Monument is made of marble.

masonry (MAY–sun–ree)
Masonry is building with stones, bricks, or blocks. The Washington Monument is a masonry tower.

obelisk (AH–buh–lisk)
An obelisk is a four-sided tower that gets smaller as it gets taller and has a point on top. The Washington Monument is an obelisk building.

quarry (KWOR–ee)
A quarry is an opening in the ground where people dig out stone for building. The stone used to build the Washington Monument came from a quarry in Maryland.

Index

Web Sites

Learn more about the Washington Monument:
http://www.nps.gov/wamo/index2.htm

Learn more about Washington, D.C.:
http://www.hswdc.org/

Learn more about George Washington:
http://www.history.org/people/washhdr.htm